# THE BRITISH SOLDIER IN THE 20TH CENTURY

Written and illustrated by

## MIKE CHAPPELL

WESSEX MILITARY PUBLISHING

Published in 1987 by
Wessex Military Publishing
1A High Street
Hatherleigh, Devon EX20 3JH
© Copyright 1987 Wessex
Military Publishing

ISBN 1 870498 00 3

Typeset and printed in Great Britain by
Toptown Printers Limited
Vicarage Lawn, Barnstaple, North Devon
England

*Front Cover:* **Private, 1st Battalion Royal Fusiliers, 24th Division, 1918. (Reconstruction).**

*Back Cover:* **Present-day infantry private wearing the load-carrying equipment at present under trial, and armed with the new 5.56mm service rifle. (MOD UKLF).**

*Right:* **Sergeant, 2nd Battalion Highland Light Infantry, Cologne, 1919. Note "cross-hatch" chevrons and ribbons of King George V Coronation Medal, Military Medal (with bar) and 1914 Star.**

# 1 : Service Dress 1902 - 1940

The field service or combat uniform worn by the British Army for the first forty years of the twentieth century was known as Service Dress. The regulations which introduced it were published in 1902 (Army Orders No. 10, 40 and 251), but in reality they formalised a dress which was already in use, particularly in the war still going on in South Africa.

There, the field uniform in which the British Army had begun the campaign (khaki drill – khaki for its sandy colour and drill for the cotton material from which it was made) had been found to give insufficient protection from the elements. Uniforms of serge – a durable twilled worsted fabric – were issued, first in the khaki colour of the cotton drill uniforms, and then in the brown, earthy, drab colour more suited to blend in with the background of the veldt. Photographs of troops in South Africa show a variety of patterns of drab serge Service Dress, both for officers and other ranks (the term for non-commissioned personnel at the time).

## Officers Uniform

The regulations of 1902 called for a uniform for officers in which the jacket was made up from "special mixture serge" the same colour as that of the other ranks, who were to have jackets of "drab mixture serge". Trousers and breeches for both officers and other ranks were to be made of "drab mixture tartan". (Tartan was the description applied to a closely-woven woollen material.)

The officers jacket was ordered to be loose-fitting except at the waist, with patch pockets on the breast and bellows pockets on the skirts below the waistband. A wide expanding pleat ran down the centre of the back and the stand-and-fall collar fastened with a hook and eye. The jacket could be lined or otherwise according to the preference of the wearer. Officers shoulderstraps were detachable, made from drab melton cloth and bore quarter-inch coloured edging according to branch of service. (Scarlet for infantry and yellow for cavalry for example. Some branches had a combination of colours.) Rank for officers up to and including Lieutenant-Colonel was indicated by a system of "crowsfeet" or "Austrian knots" in braid on the cuffs. Officers above the rank of Lieutenant-Colonel were to wear their ranking on the shoulder-

23rd Divisional Artillery, Aldershot, 1914 wearing "Kitchener blue" uniform. The man in the centre wears newly-issued – and badly fitted – Service Dress. (IWM Q 69145).

straps. Breeches were worn with puttees by officers on "dismounted" duties (i.e. those not required to ride horses), and breeches made from "Bedford cord" were worn for mounted duties with leggings and spurs. Insignia ordered to be worn by officers included both collar and cap badges (these were to be "bronzed") and buttons of regimental or corps pattern.

There is no doubt that the authorities intended Service Dress to be a "universal" field uniform, one to be worn by all regiments and corps of the British Army. The Guards were not included in the 1902 regulations but eventually adopted a distinctive Service Dress which featured – for officers – open collars, ranking worn on shoulderstraps, buttons worn in regimental groupings and non-regulation caps. Scottish infantry too refused to conform, and were to express their individuality with distinctive headdress and, in the case of the highland regiments, the continued wearing of the kilt.

It is worthwhile noting that in 1902, and for many years to come, officers

were not issued with uniform, equipment or arms, but were expected to purchase all their requirements from authorised tailors, hatters, bootmakers, etc. This meant that individual preference could be exercised in the choice of material, cut and fitting of officers uniform. In peacetime the stern eye of the Adjutant maintained standards of dress among the officers of a untit, but in wartime when inter-regimental cross-postings, difficulties in obtaining orders from tailors and the more pressing considerations of combat made dress less important, officers uniformity lapsed into the unconventional to say the least.

## Other Ranks Uniform

The Service Dress jacket for other ranks was described in the 1902 regulations as a loosely-fitting garment with a turned down "rolled" collar, rifle patches on the shoulders, patch pockets on the breast, side pockets let into the skirts below the waist and with plain, removable shoulderstraps.

A Victoria Cross investiture, France 1918. Left to right Captain J. Crowe, 2nd Worcesters; Second Lieutenant L. Knox, 150 Field Company Royal Engineers; Sergeant C. Train, 2nd London Scottish. Their uniforms typify the infantry officer, the "mounted" officer and the Highland soldier. (IWM Q 9224).

These last items were similar to those of the officers but without the coloured edging. There was a wide, false pleat down the centre of the back. Regimental and corps distinctions were shown by strips of coloured cloth on which were embroidered the titles of units. They were sewn to the sleeves of the jacket, one inch below the shoulder seam. Infantry titles were white on scarlet and had separate battalion indicators sewn below them. Cavalry titles were blue on yellow; Royal Artillery, red on dark blue; Royal Engineers, dark blue on red, and so on.

Other ranks Service Dress jackets came from the army clothing factory for issue with general service buttons attached. These had been worn by most non-commissioned ranks of the British Army since 1871, but there were exceptions, notably the cavalry, Guards, Rifles, Royal Artillery and Royal Engineers, who replaced the G.S. buttons with their own regimental pattern. Labels were sewn inside the right breast of jackets and on the left hip of trousers and breeches

to indicate the size of the garment and to assist with its fitting. Inside the right skirt of the jacket was a pocket to take the soldier's first field dressing – a first aid outfit consisting of two gauze pads with bandages. Collars fastened with hooks and eyes and there were belt hooks at the waist to support the equipment when worn. (Officers jackets, too, had these belt hooks.)

Ranking was worn on the sleeves in the traditional manner, as were badges of trade, proficiency and good conduct. These badges were usually either in drab worsted embroidery or, in some instances, metal. As in the case of officers, medal ribbons were permitted to be worn on Service Dress.

Trousers were worn by other ranks on dismounted duties. These were tucked into drab puttees wound from ankle to knee. Soldiers on mounted duties wore Bedford cord breeches with brown leather leggings. These last items were soon replaced with puttees wound from knee to ankle.

Service Dress was intended to be suitable for all extremes of temperate

climate according to how much, or how little, clothing was worn beneath it. For other ranks much of this underclothing continued to be of the pattern previously authorised including the old "greyback" flannel shirt, grey woollen socks and the dark blue wool cardigan waistcoat.

## Greatcoats and rainproofs

A greatcoat in "drab mixture milled and waterproofed cloth" was authorised for officers between 1902 and 1904. This was a double-breasted garment reaching to within a foot of the ground. Shoulderstraps as for the Service Dress jacket were worn and badges of rank were displayed upon them. The coat had turnback cuffs, a pleated back and a back strap. It was slightly modified in 1911.

The greatcoat authorised for other ranks at this time was described as "rainproof drab mixture cloth", unlined, with a cape. Single-breasted, it was similar to the blue-grey garment it replaced. By the time of the outbreak of

Sergeant, 2/1st Dorset Yeomanry, England 1916. In July 1916 this unit were ordered to hand in their horses and convert to a cyclist battalion. Our subject demonstrates the "marching order" of a cyclist, but still clings to the Service Dress of a cavalryman. Note his breeches, cavalry-style puttees and green cap band. His rifle is a P14 Enfield. (IWM Q 30428).

1st Lancashire Fusiliers, 29th Division, Somme 1916. The men wear a mixture of 1907 pattern and the 1914 "utility" pattern Service Dress. Note the Divisional signs on their sleeves and the unit insignia on their backs and helmets. (IWM Q 734).

war in 1914 greatcoats issued to other ranks were either of a dismounted or mounted pattern. Simply described these were either long single-breasted, or short double-breasted garments.

From their descriptions it will be seen that greatcoats were intended to afford protection from rain as well as cold. However, shortly after the outbreak of the Great War officers began to purchase and wear a variety of waterproof coats, particularly the "Burberry" trench coat then – as now – so popular. (Other ranks found protection from rain in the issue groundsheet which was modified in 1917 to form a cape.) At this time also officers began to purchase several semi-official patterns of greatcoat, of which one, similar to the other ranks dismounted greatcoat, gained popularity as the "British Warm", a garment which is still worn to this day.

## Footwear

Until 1902 footwear in the British Army had been made from black leather or was blackened to conform to the uniform regulations then existing. With the introduction of Service Dress brown leather was called for, the better to blend with the drab colour of the new uniform. Officers bought their boots in this colour from their bootmakers. Regulation ankle boots for other ranks were manufactured with the hide reversed and came from the factory covered in grease. This had to be laboriously removed before boots could be blackened and then polished. With the new orders they were left as they came from stores, with only the application of dubbin to maintain their waterproof quality. In time other ranks' boots took on a dirty, neutral colouring from their original yellow-tan shade.

When issued, regulation boots had steel tips on toes and heels and a row of steel studs near the toe-tip. Dismounted troops studded the complete sole, whilst mounted troops left the sole bare for better grip on stirrups.

Whilst other ranks rarely wore any other kind of footwear than the regulation ankle boot, officers adopted a wide variety of authorised and unauthorised boots and legwear with Service Dress. These included a "Field Boot", a cross between an ankle boot and a riding boot; "Trench Boots" which laced up to the knee; polo and hunting boots, and a variety of leggings and puttees.

There were several varieties of spurs worn by both officers and other ranks. These were attached to the boot by leather straps or a combination of straps and chains. A large, leather tab was usually worn on the upper spur strap to prevent the stirrup iron from cutting the laces of boots.

## Head Dress

This complicated subject is fully covered in Volume 2 of this work. However, mention should be made of the 1902 regulations as far as they covered headdress. The item for wear with Service Dress overseas was given as the "Felt hat". This had been widely worn in the South African War where it went under a number of names (Slouch hat, "Smasher", "Wide-awake", etc.). Brought back from South Africa it was worn by British units at home until replacement items were authorised and became available. For officers this was the 1902-pattern Service Dress cap, made in drab material with a brown leather chinstrap and "bronzed" cap badge and buttons.

Other ranks wore several patterns of headdress until a drab Service Dress Cap similar to the officers' pattern was

(continued on page 18)

The "utility" Service Dress. The private of the 3rd (Reserve) Battalion of the King's Own Scottish Borderers at (a) was photographed in Edinburgh in 1916. Note his Tam-o'-Shanter bonnet and the general appearance of the front of the "utility" jacket. The back of this jacket is shown at (b) and may be compared with the 1907-pattern jacket at (c). (These are badged for the 9th Rifle Brigade, 14th Division, 1916 – green and black – and the 36th Northumberland Fusiliers, 59th Division, 1918 – yellow cross, green triangle.) Details of the belt-hook are at (d); collar hooks at (e); breast pocket of the "utility" jacket at (f) for comparison with that of the 1907-pattern at (g); and the plain brass button at (h).

**During the Great War Brigadier-Generals wore the uniforms and appointments of General Officers, as shown above with the rank badge as at right. After the Great War the rank was abolished in the British Army, and was replaced with the appointment of "Colonels-Commandant" to command brigades. Eventually the commanders of brigades were given the rank of "Brigadier", with a badge of rank of a crown with three stars. They wore red cap bands and the cap badge and gorget patches formerly worn by Staff Colonels. Note the trench cap worn by our subject, pictured in 1916.**

**General Sir Edmund Allenby, commanding the Third Army of the British Expeditionary Force, France and Flanders, 1917, (Left).**

*Blunt in manner, tall, heavily-built and always impeccably turned out Allenby typified the cavalry General. Here he is portrayed in the standard General Officer's Service Dress, with its distinctive cap, gorget patches and Army commander's brassard. Note his Sam Browne belt and brace, field boots and spurs and brown leather gloves. His medal ribbons are those of the K.C.B., King George V's Coronation Medal, Queen's South African Medal, King's South African Medal and the Grand Cross of the French Legion of Honour. Shown enlarged below are the General Officer's button detail, gorget patch, metal cap badge, General's badge of rank, and a 5th Army staff brassard of late-1918. (The dark cord around Allenby's neck is that of the monocle he invariably wore.)*

**Captain, the Scots Guards, England 1939, (Right).**

*Prior to 1913 Guards officers wore step collars and ties, with their ranking on shoulderstraps (in the manner of General officers of the time) when the rest of the army was in closed collars. Other peculiarities of Guard's officers dress were the practice of wearing jacket buttons in regimental grouping, (singly for the Grenadiers, in twos for the Coldstream, in threes for the Scots, etc.) plain patch pockets, and Service Dress made from drab barathea. Our subject demonstrates all these points as well as the "plus-four" trousers and regimental headgear. His ribbons are of the General Service Medal (Palestine) and King George VI Coronation.*

**Lieutenant-Colonel, 15th Battalion Durham Light Infantry, 21st Division, France 1917, (Centre).**

*Our subject demonstrates the battle insignia of his battalion with the general appearance of the regimental officer in the line.*

**Sergeant, 2/6th King's (Liverpool Rifles), 57th (W.Lancs) Division, France 1918, (Left).**

*Little attempt was made to "smarten up" the loose and comfortable Service Dress in the early months of the Great War. Reaction to the squalor of trench life led eventually to the fashion of wearing better-fitting uniforms which were sometimes extensively tailored to produce a parade-ground appearance. This is demonstrated by our subject. The 1917-pattern "soft cap" was the preferred headgear; sometimes worn with the chin-strap artistically braided as shown. Jacket collars were tailored to a close fit, and pocket flaps were altered in imitation of those of the officers' jacket. Trousers were cut tight to the knee and puttees were wound in fancy patterns. Swagger canes were often carried by the off-duty military dandy. Many units chose to wear the embroidered titles which had been dispensed with in 1907. Below the title on our subject's right sleeve is the sign of his Division, the badge of a Lewis Gun instructor, the "crosshatch" chevrons of his badge of rank and the blue Overseas Service chevrons introduced in early 1918. (One for each year's service.) His ribbon is that of the Military Medal. Note his late-pattern boots with the crescent-shaped toecaps. Shown enlarged are his cap badge and the diamond and bar battle insignia worn on his left sleeve. (These indicated unit and company.)*

**Private, 5th (Sutherland and Caithness) Battalion, Seaforth Highlanders, 51st (Highland) Division, France 1940, (Centre).**

*Many units went to France in 1939 and 1940 clothed in Service Dress. Our subject here is typical. Note his helmet cover, No. 1 (SMLE) rifle, 1937-pattern equipment, respirator and the gas-cape rolled on his shoulders. Regimental insignia worn on his Service Dress jacket included collar badges and metal titles. These are shown enlarged.*

**Lieutenant, Royal Field Artillery, England 1902, (Right).**

*Our subject wears the first pattern of Service Dress authorised for officers by the regulations of 1902. Note his shoulderstraps and the badges of rank worn on the cuffs. Note also his breeches, leggings and spurs. His ribbon is that of the Queen's South Africa Medal. Shown enlarged are his collar badge and the details of an infantry officer's shoulderstrap.*

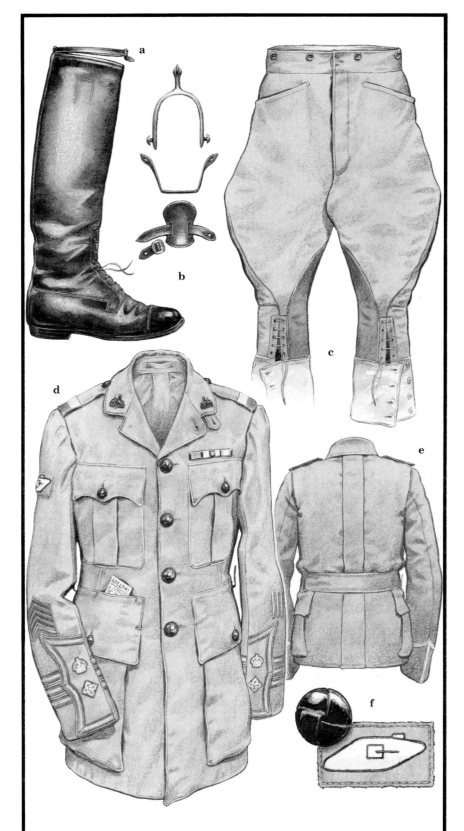

**Officer's Service Dress.** The "field boot" at (a) was designed to double as a riding or a marching boot. Shown at (b) are the component parts of a British military spur. Breeches, shown at (c), were made in drab Bedford cord or in cavalry twill in shades of khaki, fawn and even pink. They had buckskin knee grips which usually matched the colour of the breeches. At (d) is the Service Dress jacket of a Lieutenant-Colonel of the 14th Tank Corps, 1918. Note the devices for fastening the collar when worn with a PH gas helmet. Note also the green over purple shoulder slides, tank badge and leather buttons (shown in detail at (f)), ribbons of the Distinguished Service Order, Military Cross (with bar) and 1914 star, wound stripes and overseas service chevrons. At (e) is the rear of the jacket of a subaltern in a Scottish regiment, 1903.

NON-COMMISSIONED BADGES OF RANK AND APPOINTMENT (Give
as for Infantry) (a) Lance Corporal; (b) Corporal; (c) Sergeant – Rif
regiments, black on green; (d) Company Sergeant Major and Compan
Quartermaster Sergeant up to 1915. CQMS after 1915; (e) Regiment
Quartermaster Sergeant up to 1915; (f) Regimental Sergeant Major up to 1915. CSM after 1915; (g) RQMS after 1915; (h) RSM afte
1915. OFFICERS BADGES OF RANK 1902 (i) Lieutenant-Colonel; (j) Major; (k) Captain; (l) Second-Lieutenant. OFFICER
BADGES OF RANK AFTER 1902 (m) lieutenant; (n) Captain; (o) Major; (p) Colonel; (q) Second-Lieutenant, Scottish regiment
(r) Captain, Scottish regiments.

GREATCOATS (s) Other rank's dismounted pattern 1918; (t) Other rank's mounted pattern 1918 (front and rear view); (u) Officer's pattern "British Warm" 1916; (v) Officer's dismounted pattern 1911. REGULATION BOOTS (w) Late-Great War pattern ankle boot with crescent toecap shown studded for mounted duties; (x) 1914 pattern ankle boot shown studded for infantry; (y) Second-Lieutenant, 10th Argyll & Sutherland Highlanders, 32nd Division, Cologne 1919. Note the 1908-pattern marching order equipment and ashplant walking stick; (z) Private, Medical Orderly, Royal Army Medical Corps, 1918. Note the 1914-pattern marching order equipment, Good Conduct badge chevrons for more than twelve years service and two wound stripes.

a    b    c

d

Other rank's Service Dress. At (a) is the "greyback" shirt; at (b) is the dark blue cardigan; and at (c) the trousers that were standard issue with Service Dress in 1914. At (d) is the 1907-pattern jacket of a private in the 9th North Staffords, pioneer battalion 37th Division 1918. Note the gold horseshoe divisional sign with the pale-green battalion indicator below, the good conduct badge chevron (over 2 years service), the wound stripe and rifle marksman's badge. Note also the marking of the wearer's former unit, size label and pocket for the first field dressing, which is shown with the soldier's "small" or "pay" book and identity discs and bracelet.

## COLOUR PLATE C

**Colour-Sergeant, 1st Battalion, Durham Light Infantry, England 1937, (Left).**

*By the 1930s Service Dress had evolved from the loose, comfortable, but unmilitary uniform of its early years into one of the smartest outfits ever worn by the British Army. Our subject demonstrates this, turned out for a ceremonial occasion. Note his sash, white buff equipment, lanyard, medals and coloured cloth backing to the insignia worn. This includes pipeclayed badges of rank, rifle marksman's badge and the badge of best company machine gunner. His rifle is the No. 1 (SMLE). Shown enlarged are his collar badges, button detail and shoulder strap.*

**Private, 2nd Battalion, Royal Sussex Regiment, England 1904, (Centre).**

*By way of comparisons our subject wears the other rank Service Dress of its early years. His Brodrick cap has a drill cover, a neck-cloth is worn, and the old leather gaiters have yet to be replaced by puttees. Note the recently-introduced bandolier equipment, Lee-Enfield rifle, blue-grey greatcoat rolled on his back, and the ribbons of the South African War. Buttons were allowed to become dull in the field. Our subject wears three good conduct badges (chevrons) indicating over twelve years service, and the prize badge of best shot in the junior ranks of his battalion. Shown enlarged are the titles worn on his sleeves and a Brodrick cap. (In this case that of the King's Own, Royal Lancaster Regiment.) Note also the detachable shoulderstraps on our subject's jacket and the detail of the twisted shoulder cords which eventually replaced them.*

**Private, Divisional Signal Company, Royal Engineers, 55th (W.Lancs) Division, France 1917, (Right).**

*Our subject shows the back of the other ranks' Service Dress jacket. Note the false pleat, belt hooks and the double-sewn seams. Note also the red rose Divisional sign worn on the sleeves with the signaller's brassard, the yellow square battle insignia indicating his company, his shouldertitle (shown enlarged below _ Territorial/Royal Engineers/West Lancashire) and the short trousers frequently worn in summer. He signals visually with the flag he holds.*

Plate C

ROYAL SUSSEX

2

## COLOUR PLATE D

**Sergeant-Piper, 2nd Battalion Irish Guards, Guards Division, France 1917, (Right).**

*Not only the Scots wore odd variations of Service Dress. Pipers in Irish regiments wore the "caubeen" bonnet, saffron kilt and cutaway jacket. The Irish Guards dispensed with the skirt pockets on their pipers jackets and wore the titles, battalion indicators, cap badge backing, hosetops and garter flashes demonstrated by our subject. Note his 1908-pattern pistol-armed web equipment, slung box respirator and two-drone pipes. The gold stripes on his left cuff are wound stripes _ instituted in 1916. Each indicated a wound received in action.*

**Private, Animal Transport Section, 1st Battalion Royal Munster Fusiliers, 29th Division, France 1916, (Centre).**

*Our subject wears the Service Dress issued to soldiers on "mounted" duties, i.e. those connected with horses. His cap is the 1915-pattern trench cap (the "gorblimey") which bears the badge and shamrock patch of his regiment. (This is shown in detail below with the 29th Divisional sign.) He wears the "utility" jacket, Bedford cord breeches and spurs.*

**Corporal, 10th Royal Hussars (Prince of Wales's Own), England 1930s, (Left).**

*Our subject contrasts starkly with the previous figure, and demonstrates the importance attached to appearance by the peace-time, regular British Army. In the cavalry at this time "standup" collars were fashionable as were "wing" breeches. The buckskin kneegrips on breeches were frequently blancoed as were puttee tapes. The cavalry equivalent of the infantry's swagger cane was the whip, and spurs were often fitted with loose rowels that jingled as the wearer strode about. Note the cap and collar badges worn by our subject, his bandolier, lanyard and pipeclayed badges of rank. Above his chevrons are the regimental badge for Corporals and the crossed flags of an Assistant Regimental Signals Instructor. Shown in detail below are his shoulder title, Corporal's badge and cloth backing.*

Highland infantry dress was found to be impractical in the Great War. The colourful headdress and hose were replaced by drab items and kilts were covered by aprons made of heavy drab cotton (not shown here). Spats and shoes were replaced by ankle boots and short puttees. Our private of the 10th Battalion Argyll and Sutherland Highlanders was photographed at Cologne in 1919 and presents the typical appearance of the Highland soldier at war's end. Note his 1908-pattern equipment marching order, his S.M.L.E. rifle and 32nd Division battle insignia on his sleeves. (Red disc with three bars below in a colour to indicate his company.) (IWM Q 7535).

Pipe and drum Sergeants of the battalions of the 15th (Scottish) Division, France 1917. Demonstrating a fine variety of the colourful "tribal" items worn with Service Dress by Scottish infantry when putting on a show. (IWM Q 2123).

introduced in 1905. These stopgaps included the unloved "Brodrick" cap, worn with and without a drab cover; full-dress helmets, busbies and bearskins; forage caps, and the usual "tribal" headgear of the Scots.

## Overalls

Despite the fact that Service Dress was intended to be worn for all duties other than those for which full dress was worn, it was occassionally seen covered by overalls – nearly always referred to by the soldiers as "canvas" suits – for fatigues. Overalls consisted of dark brown twill jacket and trousers which faded to tan with washing. They remained on issue throughout the life of Service Dress.

## Identification

The identity of casualties could be obtained from the "small book" carried in the breast pocket of the Service Dress jacket. Regimental number, name and regiment was also marked on virtually all clothing and equipment, but in 1906 identity discs were ordered to be worn in the field, and these were supplemented by the identity bracelets, unofficial but popular, worn by troops in the Great War.

## Development of Service Dress

The year 1902 had not drawn to a close before the first change was made to Army Order No. 10. In November of that year Army Order No. 261 decreed that the system of officers' cuff ranking be replaced with flaps on which were worn the traditional badges of rank, further enhanced by chevron-lace. Ranking for all officers up to and including Colonel was to be marked in this way.

In 1904 the removeable shoulder-straps worn by both officers and other ranks were abolished and replaced by straps made of twisted cord. These were permanently attached to the jackets and fastened by a button.

In 1907 cord shoulderstraps and cloth titles were replaced for other ranks by a sewn-on cloth shoulder-strap on which metal titles were worn.

Army Order No. 279 of 1913 introduced a new Service Dress jacket for officers with an open "step" collar and with which was worn a drab shirt and tie. Skirts and side pockets on the new jacket were fuller, larger, and the back pleat was abolished. Shoulderstraps were of plain cloth similar to those on the other ranks' jacket.

By now, Service Dress had developed the general appearance that would remain for many years to come. Exceptions to the rule were the officers of the

Brigade of Guards (already mentioned) and the officers and men of the Scottish infantry. The Scots wore the Glengarry bonnet with Service Dress; adopted a "cutaway" jacket which was supposed to allow a sporran to be worn; their officers wore a different system of cuff-ranking; and the highland regiments still wore the kilt, sporran, diced hose, garters, spats and shoes in the field.

## The Great War

When war came in 1914 industry was stretched to clothe the millions of men drawn into the British Army. With drab serge material in short supply dark blue serge was used to make up uniforms for the men of Kitchener's "New Armies" in training in Great Britain. Even this expedient was insufficient in the early weeks of the war when civilian overcoats and red tunics from stores were used as stopgaps. The clothing contractors working flat out to fill orders were told to make economies and these led to "utility" patterns of other ranks jackets and greatcoats being brought into service. Turnback cuffs and rifle patches on the dismounted pattern greatcoat were dispensed with and, on the jacket, rifle patches and the false pleat back were dropped as were the pleated breast pockets. Firms making brass buttons turned out a plain

*(continued on page 24)*

(Above) Officers and men of the 7th Black Watch, 51st (Highland) Division, France 1917. The occasion was a sports meeting. Here men compete in a rifle grenade competition. Note the Service Dress distinctions worn by this battalion. (The "sporrans" are PH gas helmet haversacks.) (IWM Q 5356).

(Right) At the same meeting the Commanding officer of the 7th Black Watch confers with a Lieutenant (probably the Quartermaster) of the 5th Seaforths. Note the cut of Service Dress jackets, the Colonel's trench boots, the Lieutenant's leggings and brown leather buttons. Just visible are the two blue horizontal bars worn as battle insignia on the upper sleeve by the 7th Black Watch. (IWM Q 5359).

The many varieties of rainproof coats worn by officers from 1914 is shown top left in this 1918 group. (Note also the variety of footwear.) The preferred item was the "Burberry", an advertisement for which is shown above. The only consistent characteristic of this form of clothing was its colour, always shades of khaki or light drab. (IWM Q 11456 and courtesy of Burberry's Ltd.)

For the other ranks protection from the cold and rain was afforded by the leather jerkin, worn by the Scot at left. Note the drab serge lining and the plain, brass buttons. France, April 1918. (IWM Q 10883).

"Canvas", the name given to overalls by the Tommy, was worn over Service Dress for fatigues and training. Above, a group of a training unit of the Rifle Brigade are pictured wearing overall jackets in England in the early 1920s. Note the regimental buttons worn with the jackets, and the green-on-black chevron of the Lance-Corporal.

At right is the dismounted pattern greatcoat being worn, curiously, by a mounted soldier in 1917. Note the equipment worn, and also the trench boots of the man on the right.

Major Arthur Bles, Royal Welsh Fusiliers, Town Major of Cologne 1919. Our subject typifies the dress eccentricity of the British officer of the period. Kid gloves, polo boots, pale fawn shirt and cavalry twill breeches and monocle. Note the "flash" of his regiment and the ribbon of the French Legion of Honour. (IWM Q 7525).

The contrast between the appearance of Service Dress in the Great War and at the peak of its "smartness" is clearly shown by the photographs above. At right a private of the Army Ordnance Corps, much-wounded, wears the "utility" Service Dress with 1903-pattern bandolier equipment marching order, France 1918. (In this year his Corps was created "Royal".) At left is a private of the Gordon Highlanders in the mid-1930s. Apart from his Service Dress jacket he wears all the items of uniform associated with the pre-1914 "walking-out" full-dress. Note the Good Conduct badge, "belled" garter flashes, Slade-Wallace waistbelt and collar badges of the Scot. Note also the well-fitted and pressed appearance of his Service Dress jacket which has the cutaway skirts worn by all Scottish infantry in imitation of the pre-1914 full dress doublet.

variety, devoid of insignia, in order to cut production time. When clothing supply caught up with demand a reversion was made to the original patterns of Service Dress and the "utility" patterns were replaced as they wore out.

The war years from 1914 to 1918 saw many minor changes in Service Dress including different patterns of headgear, the introduction of short trousers in summer on the Western Front, the issue of a variety of protective clothing; but most of all the extraordinary range of items bought and worn by officers on active service. It would be no exaggeration to state that the majority of officers wore whatever was comfortable at a time when leadership came before dress discipline. Officers were sometimes ordered to wear other ranks' Service Dress to appear less conspicuous. A wide range of waterproofs and footwear were worn. Ranking was moved to shoulderstraps as German snipers began to recognise cuff ranking. Shabby jackets were patched with leather at cuff and elbow in the manner of a comfortable sports jacket; and pale fawn shirts, stocks, ties, caps, breeches and puttees were worn when out of the line. The anarchy that prevailed in officers' dress was not brought under control until well after the Armistice.

## Post-war Developments

In the early 1920s the wearing of badges of rank on cuffs by officers was abolished in favour of the wartime shoulderstrap ranking. Another wartime officers' fashion to be sanctioned at this time was that of having Service Dress made up from materials other than serge, notably the barathea of the Guards. Following yet another fashion set by the Guards, trousers cut like golfing "plus fours" became popular, whilst cavalry officers' jackets and breeches began more and more to resemble the garments seen in the hunting field.

Other ranks Service Dress was more severely regulated as the British Army became once again an all-regular force under peace-time conditions. The "soft caps" of the war years were banished in favour of a return to the wire-stiffened crowns of 1914, and in 1924 directions were issued that one of the two suits of Service Dress on issue to other ranks was to be tailored to a "better", more constricting fit. In time the military clothing factories were directed to manufacture uniform to new size

specifications designed to obtain this fit on issue.

With the decision taken not to universally issue full dress after the Great War, Service Dress became the ceremonial as well as the field service uniform for the British Army. Medals, collar badges, infantry sashes, regimental-pattern chevrons and badges, white buff and black leather equipment were all permitted to be worn with Service Dress in the 1920s in an attempt to "smarten up" what had been designed as an inconspicuous uniform. Boots were again blackened by other ranks, whose labours were eased in the early 1930s by the issue of black leather ankle boots which were neither made from reversed leather nor greased.

## The Second World War

On the outbreak of the Second World War a large part of the British Army was still clothed in Service Dress. Elements of the British Expeditionary Force were photographed in the winter of 1939/40 still in this dress. By the Spring of 1940 the B.E.F. had been issued with Battledress, but Service Dress continued to be worn by troops in garrisons in Great Britain and overseas, particularly in the Middle East. Even when Battledress had been universally issued officers were still required to provide themselves with

Service Dress which they were permitted to wear on certain specified occasions when on duty and for most off-duty events. General officers were rarely seen in the opening months of the war in any other form of uniform other than Service Dress, but after Generals of the like of Montgomery had popularised Battledress, Britain's senior officers were rarely photographed in anything else.

A "utility" officers' Service Dress, cut on the lines of that of the Guards, was authorised as the standard pattern from 1942 onwards (trousers and plain brown shoes were invariably worn with it). Another wartime expedient was the wearing of cloth belts with Service Dress by officers. Coloured field service caps were frequently worn with this form of dress also.

The story of Service Dress ends – as far as this book is concerned with the issue of Battledress as the field service uniform of the British Army in 1940, but Service Dress continued to be worn by other ranks in British service in mounted units, bands and drums, embassy staff, boys and apprentices units, military police detachments and by certain Guards Warrant Officers up until the issue of a new-pattern Service Dress in the early-1960s. Yet another "utility" pattern was manufactured during the period 1939-45, when the uniform saw its final modifications.

The Somme, 1916. Service Dress being worn for its intended purpose by men of the 1st Lancashire Fusiliers, 29th Division. The Second-Lieutenant at centre is also wearing other rank's Service Dress. Note the 1908-pattern "battle-order" equipment, bandoliers of extra ammunition, PH gas helmets in their cotton haversacks, digging tools and the 29th Division's battle insignia on sleeves, backs and helmets. This platoon fixes bayonets before moving to the jump-off point for the great assault of 1st July. Most men in the picture subsequently became caualties.